Vintage Floral Fantasy

Grayscale Adult Coloring Book

Olde Glorie Studios

Copyright 2016
Olde Glorie Studios
All Rights Reserved

LILIUM AURATUM.

LILIUM AURATUM.

ALSTROEMERIA CHILENSIS, VARR.

ALSTROEMERIA CHILENSIS. VARR.

www.ingramcontent.com/pod-product-compliance
Lightning Source LLC
Chambersburg PA
CBHW080712190526
45169CB00006B/2346